Spiritual Than God

Michael Yaw Tano

Published by Return to Christ, 2023.

SPIRITUAL THAN GOD

First edition. February 27, 2023.

Copyright © 2023 Michael Yaw Tano.

ISBN: 979-8215250792

Written by Michael Yaw Tano.

Also by Michael Yaw Tano

Until Sin Becomes Bitter
Come Home, Lost Wanderer
Spiritual Than God

Watch for more at https://www.miketano.wordpress.com.

Table of Contents

Acknowlegement

I'm grateful to God for leading and guiding me to write this book.

Thanks to Reverend Jones Clifford Akosa.

Thanks to Reverend Samuel Agyenim Boateng.

Thanks to Rev. John Kofi Bosomtwe.

Thanks to Rev. John Kwabena Boachie and all A.G.T.S. faculty members.

Thanks to Rev. Emmanuel Darku and all pastors in the Asokore Mampong District.

Thanks to my seminary mates, especially the A.G.T.S. class of 2020.

INTRODUCTION

Maybe you are shocked about the theme of this writing. I do not want you to be! In this life, we can trace from the outset when humankind fell from grace and see that humanity has tried so many times to be very spiritual than God. It is not a fanciful tale and a story to scorn after, rather a reality that should make us all mourn and re-examine our lives. It is very easy and common to live and behave as though you are more spiritual than God. How can one be more spiritual than his Creator, who is all-wise and all-powerful? It is up to you and me to figure out how we can act more spiritually than God in the pages of this brief discourse.

Holier than thou was born because of behaving and acting spiritually superior to God. If we know God and respect his standards, we will never act spiritually superior to Him. If we understand the consequences of acting as if we are more spiritual than He is, we will never board the spiritual-than-God train. From the onset, the creation has acted as if it is more spiritual than the Creator. From the beginning of human history, the heart of man has been found in this place several times.

Therefore, I wish to travel with you, as we will discover in this book what to be more spiritual than God means and how many in the past have boarded this heretical train. I have themed this book ***"SPIRITUAL THAN GOD,"*** because it is so rampant in human history, and even today, we see this going on in our lives. Let us find some people who lived before us and behaved and acted to be more spiritual than God and how some in our generation are walking on that same road. Though those who preceded us had many of them who behaved as though they were more spiritual than God, to be frank, I can only talk about a few to solidify my claim. I believe you will be blessed with this book. May the Lord help us in this endeavor! Amen.

Your Servant,
Michael Yaw Tano

CENTRAL TRUTH

But He gives a greater grace. Therefore, *it* says, "God is opposed to the proud, but gives grace to the humble." James 4:6NASB.

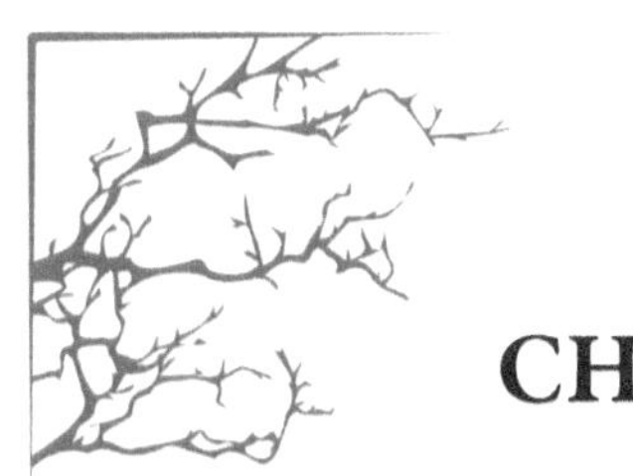

CHAPTER ONE

FIRST CHARACTER-—LUCIFER

EVIL CAME OUT OF SATAN. He was not always Satan. There was a time when he was called Lucifer. He was a servant of God who was pure and holy and perfect before God, his Father. Satan was one of God's cherubs. He obeyed God for some time until iniquity was found in him. The scripture expressly says:

How you are fallen from heaven, O Lucifer, son of the morning! How you are cut down to the ground-mighty though you were against the nations of the world. **13** For you said to yourself, 'I will ascend to heaven and rule the angels. I will take the highest throne. I will preside on the Mount of Assembly far away in the north. **14** I will climb to the highest heavens and be like the Most High.' **15** But instead, you will be brought down to the pit of hell, down to its lowest depths. **16** Everyone there will stare at you and ask, "Can this be the one who shook the earth and the kingdoms of the world? **17** Can this be the one who destroyed the world and made it into a shambles, who demolished its greatest cities and had no mercy on his prisoners?" Isa 14:12-17TLB.

Concerning this text, one writer argues:

These verses also have a double application. They are still part of the proverb against the king of Babylon. The language, however, shows that he is a type of Satan. Lucifer means "Light Bearer." ... Satan was once an angel called Lucifer, who, in love with his own beauty, fell into pride and self-centeredness. (Nelson, 2002, p. 891)

Although scholars are divided concerning this text, the popular opinion is what Nelson has suggested. To this end, I will follow the popular opinion regarding the above passage. The text applies to both the king of Babylon and Satan. As seen above, the sin that was found in Lucifer and brought about his demotion was pride. Satan thought he was more spiritual than God and thought of himself as holier than the King of Kings and the Lord of Lords. His heart was lifted up because of his beauty and perfection. He decided to set his seat on high and make himself equal to God. He thought he could do better than what God was doing. He thought he could offer better judgment than what the Most High is doing. This deadly sin was found in Lucifer. The anointed cherub forsook his state and coveted things that belonged to God alone. He did not keep his place but rather wanted the seat of God himself. Isn't this clear evidence that Satan was telling God through his actions that he was more spiritual and holier than the glorious King?

His actions are evidence of his intent. He wanted the seat of God. He desired to be the ultimate judge and ruler! He wanted to receive the glory that was due to God. He wanted all that is named God to be his subject. This is what made him Satan. When he corrupted his nature and character, the name Satan suited him better than Lucifer. This is the origin of all evil. It proceeded from an act of disobedience, covetousness, and pride. From this single act of disobedience, all that we see in our world sprouts out. When one departs from the simplicity that is in God and covets after God, deciding to fight God for His seat, we should be aware that the outcome will not be pleasing. How can the potter and the clay fight? Is the potter not superior to the clay? The potter and the clay fought, and the clay was defeated. His (Lucifer's) demotion humbled him. He has since been an enemy of the Creator. The devil has fought every single idea of the Potter because he does not think that the Potter is judging and ruling as He should. He believes he can do better than that. He thinks he knows better than the creator.

Lucifer defiled his garment because he thought he was more spiritual than God. His beauty deceived him, and his perfection did not continue, for God stripped him of it. His beauty and perfection were therefore tainted. All that was good in him became corrupted, and he did not return to the place that he used to have in the presence of God. His seat, which belonged to him, was taken from him by an angel of God. He became hostile toward the things that pertain to God. His doom has been declared from of old. There will be no light in the end. He will suffer harm because he has challenged his Creator. He did not treat the Creator with the respect that He deserved.

If one is separated from God, what do you think happens? I believe that those who have been separated from God grow and mature in their craftiness. All their actions and deeds are toward sin. Each step they take distances them from God and lead them to become more wicked, hostile, and misbehaving. How the mighty fall! Lucifer turned against his Lord and God because he wanted to be like the Most High. He wanted all the angels to worship him as they worship the Most High. Isn't this being more spiritual than God and holier than thou? This nature, habit, and character did not proceed from mankind but rather from the devil, who was called Lucifer.

Even though he sinned and God expelled him from heaven, he retains his power. He can cause harm if you are without God. He can trouble you. The heavens shook in the days of Job. Yes, he was able to do that! There is no good in him anymore except wickedness. After he was cast down, he still wanted the throne of God. As a matter of fact, he still thinks that he can fight against the King of Kings and the Lord of Lords and conquer Him. For this reason, Christ came! Christ came to destroy the work of the devil and, in so doing, defeat the enemy. The scripture says:

Having canceled out the certificate of debt consisting of decrees against us *and* which was hostile to us; and He has taken it out of the way, having nailed it to the cross. When He had disarmed the rulers and authorities, He made a public display of them, having triumphed over them through Him. Col 2:14-15NASB

He did not only cancel the certificate but also make a public display of the devil and his troops. Christ has shamed the devil. Yet Satan still believes that he will be able to fight God. When you go far from God, delusion becomes your friend and close acquaintance. The final battle that will be hosted in Armageddon will see to it that Satan and his forces have been defeated once and for all. They will all be cast into the lake that burns and cannot be quenched by sand or water. Satan, together with the one-third of the angels that he was able to win to his side, will not be able to run from this fatal fate and judgment.

This is the result of believing that you are more spiritual and holier than God. The doom of the earth started from this act that Lucifer committed, and this plague continues to injure and affect us daily. We see that the mother of sin is unbelief, but what is the mother of unbelief? Unbelief arose from the idea of being more spiritual than God and holier than He is. This is where unbelief was born. If you think that you are more spiritual than God, will you adhere to His precepts? I believe not! You do not follow His rules because you believe you can do better than He does; how can you then follow His precepts? So when spiritual than God comes into a display, then unbelief is what follows. When unbelief has come in, then all the other sins follow and ruin your conscience, heart, and mind. You become vile, and sin becomes your friend. You begin to cherish sin and treasure it.

That was how Satan began, and now he is not only called the old serpent but rather the dragon. He has grown and matured in his sins. He is the father of all lies and fabrications. He has deceived many a soul and taken them into slavery. It started when Satan thought he was more spiritual than God. May we not be negligent when we see this in our hearts! We need to fight sin from its beginning before it matures in our hearts and takes us to a place where we can never return. If care is taken, we will not go to this place of doom but rather grow in Christ and know the worth of holiness and find the joy of living holily and in sanctity.

If it were possible for Lucifer to corrupt his beauty and defile his garment, then, sirs, we need to take heed to our own souls and be diligent in this endeavor. We need to be careful not to fall for the deception and the short-term pleasures that sin will present to us. On the other hand, let us think carefully about the consequences of our one error. Lucifer only committed one error, and he became Satan. It is the small sins that we are negligent of that take us to a place of doom. May we receive mercy and grace to walk in this life of many sins without defiling our garments and corrupting our beauty in Christ! Amen

Let us pray: Gracious Lord, our heart is deceitful, and it is written not only in thy word but also in our daily lives and living, that we bear witness to the fact of the heart's wickedness. So easily and our hearts are puffed up, as though we do not need you. Yes, so easily, we assume we can manage without you, Lord; please help us! Help us not to think as Satan thought and, in the end, suffered harm. Help our immortal souls and change our hearts so that we can desire, gasp, and pant after you every day. We know that you are the Lord, who is merciful and gracious and full of love; for this reason, help us, Lord, and make a name for yourself; in the name of Christ, we ask you for these things. Amen

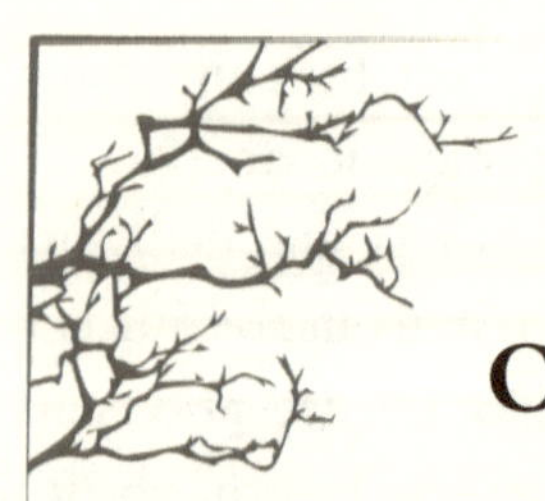

CHAPTER TWO

SECOND CHARACTERS-—ADAM AND EVE

ADAM AND HIS WIFE THOUGHT they knew better than God, and in so doing, they were deceived by the devil. I want to propose two ideas that show that Adam and Eve thought they were more spiritual than God. The first was that they thought they could replace God with something else! And on a second note, Adam and his wife, Eve, played a blame game instead of accepting their faults. Let's talk about these two acts of Adam and Eve and see how they acted as though they were better than God.

<u>Replacing God</u>

God created Adam and Eve; they were created to desire only the Creator and pant after Him. They were to be satisfied by the creator! The Creator was the one who should have satisfied their longing souls. His presence should have been their comfort and delight. But mankind sought another satisfaction that was outside of God. Mankind thought they knew better than their Creator, who created the heart in such a way that it would be satisfied with only Him (God). When mankind sought after other things to bring satisfaction, they broke God's heart. This summarized mankind's story:

> And the Lord was sorry that He had made man on the earth, and He was grieved in His heart. Gen 6:6NASB

The Lord was grieved and was sorry that created man. It did not start in the time of Noah but rather in the time of Adam. The Scripture again says:

Now the serpent was more crafty than any beast of the field which the Lord God had made. And he said to the woman, "Indeed, has God said,

'You shall not eat from any tree of the garden'?" **2** And the woman said to the serpent, "From the fruit of the trees of the garden we may eat; **3** but from the fruit of the tree which is in the middle of the garden, God has said, 'You shall not eat from it or touch it, lest you die.'" **4** And the serpent said to the woman, "You surely shall not die! **5** "For God knows that in the day you eat from it your eyes will be opened, <u>and you will be like God, knowing good and evil</u>." **6** When the woman saw that the tree was good for food, and <u>that it was a delight to the eyes, and that the tree was desirable to make *one* wise</u>, she took from its fruit and ate; and she gave also to her husband with her, and he ate. **7** Then the eyes of both of them were opened, and they knew that they were naked; and they sewed fig leaves together and made themselves loin coverings. Gen 3:1-7NASB (emphasis mine)

The Lord's heart was broken by the disobedience of Adam and his wife. Henceforth, the posterity of man will wallow in sin. This is why the Lord was grieved that He made man. Eve and her husband coveted something that should not have been coveted. They did not like their first place of living for God and in his presence. Mankind wanted to be like God. Is this not clear that mankind thought that they knew better than their Creator? The eyes of Eve coveted that which God had specifically told them not to eat. The woman and her husband wanted wisdom, but the Lord saw that it was not fit to be given to them this kind of wisdom.

Mankind thought they knew better, and what God withheld, mankind went and took it. The graceless wisdom was taken by them, and the cup that contained it was emptied because mankind drank the knowledge of good and evil from it. But was this going to satisfy mankind? No way! The scripture says, "He has also set eternity in their heart" (Eccl 3:11 NASB). God has set eternity in the heart of man. If we want satisfaction, we can only find it in God. Only God can provide us with peace, comfort, and rest. When mankind sought different things to offer satisfaction, their woes began.

Our first parents were given a garden in the city of Eden. They had peace and comfort. Everything was perfect. God walked in their midst, but they did not see the worth of His presence. They traded the presence of God for food because they thought they knew better than God. They treated the presence of God with contempt. They thought they were more spiritual than him. This is what brought us misery and sorrow. If we behave as though we are more spiritual than Him, our Creator will not be our friend, and sorrow will be our close acquaintance.

If our first parents had been content with what God had given them, the misery would not have come. If they had not behaved as though they were more spiritual than God and knew better than Him who created them, they would have maintained their peace. A single act of disobedience has cost their posterity much more than they imagined. If they look back and see what the decision has done to their posterity, they will be sorrowful and mournful. They will not be pleased with themselves for acting spiritually superior to Him.

Man coveted the supremacy of God. Man desired to be God! Man did not want his position but coveted the throne of God! As Satan tried and fell from grace, so did he deceive man to try and take what he couldn't take, namely, the seat of God. We saw earlier that Satan coveted the throne of God and suffered demotion; since it was he who deceived man, Satan went for the same throne through mankind. He did not give up fighting. Since the first war was fought concerning who sits on God's throne from the beginning, it has continued to all ages.

In the heavenly places, the war was fought. On earth, it has continued! The first war was fought when Satan wanted, if possible, to dethrone God or be equal with God. Satan has always coveted the throne of God and will do so until his last breath. Since he prospered in deceiving mankind into coveting the throne of God, Satan has fought God through mankind ever since.

The warfare has always been about one thing: Satan is after the throne of God! He wants to exalt himself to the level of God. This is what his heart desires. Adam and Eve were deceived by the devil into thinking that they could be like God. He deceived them, and they lost the glory that was their covering. They became like any other creature! They became helpless, miserable, and graceless. When they decided to go for something to satisfy their longing soul apart from the Lord, they brought on themselves their own sorrow and misery. They injured themselves and brought a thorn into their own flesh. They were banished from their small paradise. They were banished from the city of comfort. They clothed themselves with ignominy. Imagine the shame that stayed with them. Anytime that one looks into the face of the other, they remembered what they did in Eden. This is the consequence of trying to be more spiritual than your Creator.

If Adam and Eve had not gone for the throne of God and coveted the place of God, they would have maintained their peace. If they had only enjoyed the presence of God as the only thing that could satisfy their longing souls, their comfort would not have been taken from them. They lost their satisfaction and their city because of fruit. They wanted to be like God, and in this act of treachery and treason, they were sent to this place of much toil and hardship. Suffering became their brother, and ignominy and ignoble things became their possession.

Can mankind and other mortals know better than their Creator? Isn't it funny how we are easily deceived when we are exalted? Satan was once perfect, and he thought he could take the throne of God. Adam and Eve enjoyed intimacy with God, and they never longed for the presence of God because their thirst was always quenched, and they thought they could be like Him and find another means apart from God to satisfy their longing. How easily we digress from the narrow path, which has a small door.

They were evicted from the garden as a result of their disobedience. They called upon themselves woes. Because of sin, Adam and Eve lost their second son to murder and their first son to a curse. This is the true nature of sin. If we do not enjoy God and live under his umbrella, we will suffer harm. We will not live in peace; rather, chaos will greet us daily.

THE BLAME GAME

"Who told you that you were naked? Have you eaten from the tree of which I commanded you not to eat?" **12** And the man said, "The woman whom Thou gavest *to be* with me, she gave me from the tree, and I ate." **13** Then the Lord God said to the woman, "What is this you have done?" And the woman said, "The serpent deceived me, and I ate."

Gen 3:11-13NASB

When they sinned and God came to them, God asked Adam where he was. Adam responded by saying that he and his wife were hiding because they were naked. Upon this, the Lord further asked Adam, "How did you know that you're naked?" Then another question followed! Whether or not they ate the forbidden fruit. Instead of saying "yes" or "no," the blame game started! Adam shifted responsibility to his wife. Instead of accepting the wrong, the first act of disobedience in the history of mankind brought what is called "holier than thou." Adam thought he was holier than the woman because it was the woman who was deceived first. He thought he was better than his wife. Adam was playing the blame game at the time, rather than accepting their mistake.

On the other hand, Eve, Adam's wife, decided to continue the blame game. She also shifted the blame to the serpent! Since the serpent is referred to as Satan, he was not able to shift the blame on anyone since if he attempted that, he would accuse God of his error. The devil, therefore, knew that it was his own heart that deceived him, and for that reason, he could not shift any blame.

When Adam and Eve thought they were more spiritual than God, it brought "holier than thou"! As we have seen that spiritual than God is the contempt of man against his Creator, holier than thou is the contempt of man against man. We have seen the manifestation of "holier than thou" throughout human history. Adam's descendants have shown and demonstrated this in both words and deeds. Adam thought he was holier than Eve, and Eve also thought she was holier than the serpent, and that is how the blame game was born in Eden. Instead of accepting our wrongs, we choose to shift blame and assume we are better than our colleagues. That is how our first parents behaved.

If the mistake had been accepted by our parents, maybe we would have had a different case on our hands. This should tell the Christian reader that, if Lucifer and our first parents could fall from grace to grass, we should be careful lest we fall from grace too. We should not trust in the mere "professionism" in our day and simple "believism" which have become the norm of our day. It is the combination of genuine faith in Christ and the fruit of repentance that shows that a person is saved. If our faith is without the fruit of repentance, we should be careful, for even demons have faith. May the Lord help us not to fall from grace! Amen.

Let's Pray: Ah Lord, it is You alone who is our King, and it is in You alone we trust! We trust in Your sovereignty to lead us in all our endeavors so that we may not fall short of the grace that You have provided for us in Christ. Help us so that we may not stumble as our first parents did! Help us not to trust in our own hands to provide us with salvation. Lord, help us that we may not continue in the folly of our first parents, who neglected Thee, who is the fountain of life for broken cisterns. O, You alone are the source of our satisfaction, and we gasp and yearn after you. Satisfy us, Lord, and let us see that it is only You that we need to encounter true satisfaction. Amen

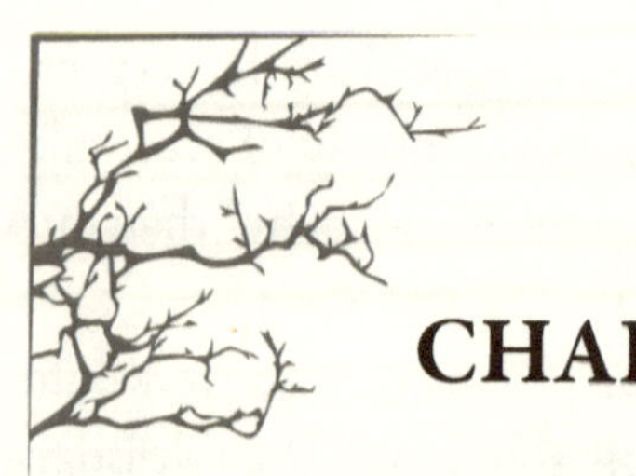

CHAPTER THREE

THIRD CHARACTER-—CAIN

I'D LIKE US TO LOOK at the story of Cain and his brother Abel, and how Cain demonstrated through his actions that he was both more spiritual than God and holier than his brother Abel. The scripture for this story says:

So it came about in the course of time that Cain brought an offering to the Lord of the fruit of the ground. 4 And Abel, on his part also brought of the firstlings of his flock and of their fat portions. And the Lord had regard for Abel and for his offering: 5 but for Cain and for his offering He had no regard. So Cain became very angry and his countenance fell. 6 Then the Lord said to Cain, "Why are you angry? And why has your countenance fallen? 7 "If you do well, will not *your countenance* be lifted up? And if you do not do well, sin is crouching at the door; and its desire is for you, but you must master it." 8 And Cain told Abel his brother. And it came about when they were in the field, that Cain rose up against Abel his brother and killed him. 9 Then the Lord said to Cain, "Where is Abel your brother?" And he said, "I do not know. Am I my brother's keeper?" 10 And He said, "What have you done? The voice of your brother's blood is crying to Me from the ground. 11 And now you are cursed from the ground, which has opened its mouth to receive your brother's blood from your hand. Gen 4:3-11NASB (emphasis mine)

The Christian reader should know that where sin abounds, curses abound. How does this story show that Cain was acting more spiritually than God, and what can we learn from this story in this endeavor?

When Cain and Abel had both presented their sacrifice to the Lord, was it not up to the Lord to decide to either accept their offering or reject it? Is it not the prerogative of the Lord to either accept or reject their sacrifice; what then is the cause for Cain's displeasure? When the Lord accepted Abel's offering, Cain became angry and struck him to death. Cain killed his younger brother because Abel presented an acceptable offering to the Lord.

The Lord decided to choose Abel's offering over Cain's offering, so why did he strike his younger brother? Is this not clear that Cain was not angry about his brother but that his main displeasure was against God? Did Abel ask the Lord to reject his brother's offering? If he didn't, why did Cain strike him to death? Cain was telling God in his actions that he (Cain) is more spiritual than Him. He thought the Lord was being unfair by not accepting his sacrifice.

In this, Cain thought that if he were God, he would have done better than what the Almighty did. In this, he was very angry with God. Cain was very disappointed in God. If God was with him, physically, he would have struck Him first. His rage was directed at the Omnipotent and Sovereign God! From the actions of Cain, it was clear that he was telling God what offerings to accept and what should be rejected. He insulted the wisdom of his creator. Is this not what clothed man after he corrupted his glory with sin? If the glory departs, what do you think will happen then? The eventualities are what we are seeing! Brothers, without God, we are doomed forever!

This act of Cain happened right after the disobedience of our first parents. Sin became the norm of the day. The heart of man darkened, and it fought against its Creator from every angle. Man had nothing that could be called good. The heart of man became sick and vile, deceitful and wicked. The heart became hostile to the things of God, and this is evident as seen in this story. Cain's heart was found to be not only more spiritual than God but also holier than his brother. If Cain knew that his brother did not ask God to accept his offering and yet went ahead and killed him, was Cain not telling God that he was holier than his brother? Is this not why he struck him to death? Cain's rage was directed first at God for not accepting his offering, and then at his own brother because he thought he was better and holier than his brother, and the Lord accepted his (Abel's) offering instead.

Cain was warned earlier that sin was crouching at his door and should master it. Yet, Cain thought he did not need any warnings and alarms from God. He thought he was sufficient and could handle anything that comes his way. Instead of trusting in the Lord, Cain rejected the warning and suffered harm. Sin mastered Cain and took him to a desolate place. Cain was cursed because sin took hold of him. He couldn't master sin as his parents couldn't and were cursed, so he too was cursed!

Let's pray: Father, You made it known to Cain that sin crouched at his door, yet he did not hearken! We beseech You not to let us fall prey to the enemy and become his subjects. Help us so that we may be able to gain mastery over sin, but not otherwise. Help us not to think that we know better than You and suffer harm. Gracious Lord, your security is our hope, and your love is our strength! Shield us from the error of Cain and grace our hearts to love You and our neighbors. We bless You for the answered prayer. Amen

CHAPTER FOUR

FOURTH CHARACTER-—PEOPLE OF BABEL

And it came about as they journeyed east, that they found a plain in the land of Shinar and settled there. **3** and they said to one another, "Come, let us make bricks and burn *them* thoroughly." and they used brick for stone, and they used tar for mortar. **4** and they said, "Come, let us build for ourselves a city, and a tower whose top *will reach* into heaven, and let us make for ourselves a name; lest we be scattered abroad over the face of the whole earth." **5** and the LORD came down to see the city and the tower which the sons of men had built. **6** and the LORD said, "Behold, they are one people, and they all have the same language. And this is what they began to do, and now nothing which they purpose to do will be impossible for them. **7** come, let US go down and there confuse their language, that they may not understand one another's speech." **8** so the LORD scattered them abroad from there over the face of the whole earth; and they stopped building the city. **9** therefore its name was called babel, because there the LORD confused the language of the whole earth; and from there the LORD scattered them abroad over the face of the whole earth. Gen 11:2-9NASB

WHEN GOD CREATED MANKIND, He said to Adam and Eve: "Be fruitful and multiply, and fill the earth, and subdue it; and rule over the fish of the sea and over the birds of the sky, and over every living thing that moves on the earth." **29** Then God said, "Behold, I have given you every plant yielding seed that is on the surface of all the earth, and every tree which has fruit yielding seed; it shall be food for you; **30** and to every beast of the earth and to every bird of the sky and to every thing that moves on the earth which has life, *I have given* every green plant for food "; and it was so" (Gen 1:28-30 NASB). The very purpose of man was to be fruitful, multiply, and fill the earth. This very purpose of God was hanging in the air at Babel. The thing they were playing with had a divine purpose! They were fighting the will of God. In their wickedness, they did not want to scatter on the face of the earth as the Lord had said they should.

When these people decided to build a tower for themselves so that they would no longer move an inch from Babel, their actions demonstrated that they were more spiritual than God, and as a result, they challenged God to act. God had to come down to thwart their plans so that His plan could be revealed.

The people of Babel wanted to confine themselves there and leave the rest of the earth to rot! In unity, they stood against God. In unity, they fought His will for mankind. You see, in the same way, this generation has done so. In unity, the will of God for mankind is being fought daily by some governments. God's purpose for marriage is what many have discarded. Our generation is acting similarly to the people of Babel. What was an abomination has now been branded as good. Yes, evil has been branded and tagged as good. Homosexuality and lesbianism have become legal! Is this not so in our generation? In unity, the people of the earth are fighting the will of God. The very fabric of sanctity and morality is at stake! Our generation has fought against the very purpose of God for man.

As the people of Babel tried to forfeit the purpose of God for their lives to fill the earth, we have done worse in our generation. Many children are being killed daily in the womb by wicked men and women. Is abortion not what we are seeing in our day? Will the wrath of God not come upon this wicked and abominable generation? Will his anger and fury not fall on this generation? If He descended and confused those who were in Babel, will He stand by and applaud this generation for this wickedness and lawlessness in our generation? Nay! He will descend with His angels, and doom will clothe those who lived outside His will. As He confused the people of old, so will He do the same to this abominable generation. I will talk about this more later!

When the people of Babel tried to be more spiritual than Him, they saw Him descending. He did not descend to applaud them for their technological advancement. Though in their time, they were advanced in knowledge, which is why they were able to build that tower to the level they reached. They did not receive applause because their knowledge was being used foolishly. It was used to fight the will of God for mankind. Is this generation not treading on the same road that those people in the days of old did? The people of Babel thought they did not need to scatter across the face of the earth, but that was the will of God for their lives. They thought they knew better than God. For this, God had to confound them and their language!

As we have seen in previous chapters, all those who acted as if they were more spiritual than God were punished. Satan was demoted and cursed; Adam was demoted and cursed; and Cain was cursed and separated from his family. This is the consequence of being more spiritual than God. This happened to the people of Babel too! They were confused. They were separated from their family. They used to speak the same language at first, but when they tried to be more spiritual than God, He confounded their language, which brought separation. In this, I can say that many were separated from their families, some from their friends and neighbors. May we not head down this road of being more spiritual than God or being more holy than our brother! Amen

Let us pray: Oh Lord, we give thanks to You! Lord, help us not to fight your will for our lives. Help us to follow You in every way and tune our spirits to hear from you daily. Confound anything in our lives that appears to be more spiritual than You are, and have Your way in our lives. It is better to be confounded now than to be confounded on judgment day. For this reason, we pray thee, arise and deliver us from our own stupidity of heart and turn us to Yourself. We praise you in Christ our Lord. Amen

CHAPTER FIVE

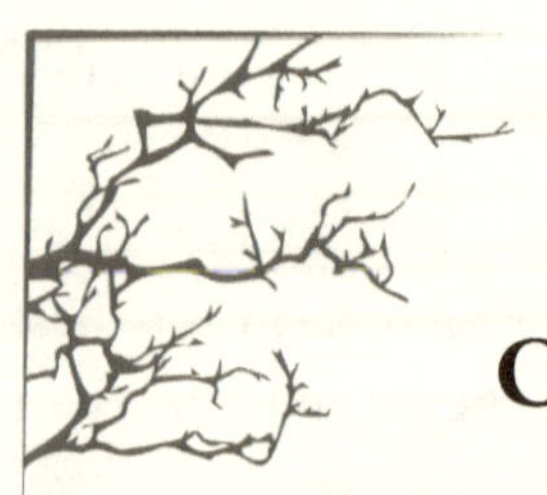

FIFTH CHARACTER-—KING SAUL

I DO WISH TO PROPOSE two ways in which I believe King Saul overstepped and thought he was more spiritual than God. These two propositions are;

- Making an Unjustified Sacrifice
- Leaving King Agag and some of the animals alive

<u>Making an Unjustified Sacrifice</u>

When the Israelites asked God for a king, that was the day God drew a clear line between those whom He has chosen to minister to His people and those who will minister to Him directly. The kings were to minister to the people directly, and the priests and prophets were also to minister to God. In the days of old, it was only the prophet who stood and ministered to the people and God directly. There was only one office, and that was the office of the prophet. The prophet was both a king and a minister of God. That's how God designed it. This is how Eli lived his life. He served as both a priest and a king for God's people. This is what Samuel came to continue. It started when God was bringing them out of the land of Egypt. The Prophet Moses was both their spiritual and physical leader. It was the prophets and priests who held this position as leaders. After Moses died, Joshua filled the gap left by Moses and continued to be their spiritual leader.

This was the life of the Israelites. God was ruling over them through His prophets and priests. It was rather unfortunate that the people of Israel compared themselves to other nations. And when they made comparisons, they went to God for a king. They did not like God ruling over them directly. They wanted a human king who would lead them to war as other nations had. This is where King Saul comes in. He became the first King of Israel. A time came when the people of Israel were at war, and the Scripture says: Now he waited seven days, according to the appointed time set by Samuel, but Samuel did not come to Gilgal; and the people were scattering from him. 9 So Saul said, "Bring to me the burnt offering and the peace offerings." And he offered the burnt offering. 10 And it came about as soon as he finished offering the burnt offering, that behold, Samuel came; and Saul went out to meet him *and* to greet him. 11 But Samuel said, "What have you done?" And Saul said, "Because I saw that the people were scattering from me, and that you did not come within the appointed days, and that the Philistines were assembling at Michmash, 12 therefore I said, 'Now the Philistines will come down against me at Gilgal, and I have not asked the favor of the Lord.' So I forced myself and offered the burnt offering." 13 And Samuel said to Saul, "You have acted foolishly; you have not kept the commandment of the Lord your God, which He commanded you, for now the Lord would have established your kingdom over Israel forever. 14 But now your kingdom shall not endure. 1 Sam 13:8-14 NASB

King Saul seemed to be unaware of the separation that God had established between the two offices of kings and prophets. Saul thought he could do the work of the prophet and, in his ignorance, tried to combine what God had separated. Saul had no idea that no man on earth was allowed to combine these things that God had separated. It was only Christ Jesus who would again join the two offices together in

His kingdom. It is only He who will be both King, Prophet, and High Priest.

In God's eyes, what Saul did was a greater sin than we realize. Do we assume that it was a small sin? If it was, King Saul would have had a second chance, but right after he committed this sin, his kingdom was said to not endure, and a man was coming after him whom God has sought and is after His own heart. This is the weight of his sin. He tried to be more spiritual than God, and he did what was abominable in the sight of God. As in the days of old, when the two sons of Aaron lit a strange fire, so did Saul sacrifice a strange offering. The fire consumed the two sons of Aaron, but the fury of God was upon Saul, and it terminated his kingdom that day.

Who can comprehend the gravity of being more spiritual than God? Who can compute its punishment? Oh, brothers, we need to be vigilant and examine our lives and our ways if we are trying to be more spiritual than God in any way. A lack of knowledge is not an excuse for our sin and error! Let us, therefore, feed our souls with the truth of God, lest we suffer the fate of Saul.

<u>LEAVING KING AGAG AND SOME OF THE ANIMALS ALIVE</u>

Again, King Saul continued his adventure of rebellion against God. He was sent on a mission to massacre the whole city, but he did not. This passage narrates the story as it happened:

Then the word of the Lord came to Samuel, saying, **11** "I regret that I have made Saul king, for he has turned back from following Me, and has not carried out My commands." And Samuel was distressed and cried out to the Lord all night. **12** And Samuel rose early in the morning to meet Saul; and it was told Samuel, saying, "Saul came to Carmel, and behold, he set up a monument for himself, then turned and proceeded on down to Gilgal." **13** And Samuel came to Saul, and Saul said to him, "Blessed are you of the Lord! I have carried out the command of the Lord." **14** But Samuel said, "What then is this bleating of the sheep in my ears, and the lowing of the oxen which I hear?" **15** And Saul said, "They have brought them from the Amalekites, for the people spared the best of the sheep and oxen, to sacrifice to the Lord your God; but the rest we have utterly destroyed." **16** Then Samuel said to Saul, "Wait, and let me tell you what the Lord said to me last night." And he said to him, "Speak!" **17** And Samuel said, "Is it not true, though you were little in your own eyes, you were *made* the head of the tribes of Israel? And the Lord anointed you king over Israel, **18** and the Lord sent you on a mission, and said, 'Go and utterly destroy the sinners, the Amalekites, and fight against them until they are exterminated.' **19** "Why then did you not obey the voice of the Lord, but rushed upon the spoil and did what was evil in the sight of the Lord?" 1 Sam 15:10-19NASB

After trying to combine what God had separated, again, King Saul thought he was more spiritual than God in the sense of refusing to exterminate the entire nation. When he went there, he and his people took the sheep that were fat. He thought God cherished sacrifice over obedience, and in this, he wronged God again. He sealed his faith in this act. Obeying is preferable to sacrificing, which King Saul was unaware of. He thought God dwells in heaven and enjoys the burnt offerings of men more than the obedience of men.

What is needful was neglected by Saul, and he paid greatly. His kingdom was torn asunder when he chose sacrifice over obedience. He thought he was more spiritual than God in the sense that he found it difficult to slaughter those whom God had ordered him to. He showed mercy where God had already shown His anger. God's justice was upon them, and King Saul went there with mercy. Saul justified what God had already condemned. Can we tell the Lord not to judge? Is it not in His right and power to judge and condemn? If He is the sole person in the whole universe who has this sovereign power, why does King Saul rob God of His authority?

Refusing to massacre the entire people and their animals was an act of trying to be more spiritual than God, and in this, God did not take it easy. The anger of the Lord was kindled against King Saul, and He tore apart the kingdom of Saul once and for all. The Amalekites were God's enemies. He declared that He would destroy them because they inflicted injury and harm on the Israelites when they were coming from Egyptian captivity. Saul thwarted the plans of God when he left Agag alive. He insulted God such that He would be considered a liar. This is why God did not take Saul's sin lightly.

Should this not ring a bell? We should be careful, for the heart is deceitful. So easily, we think highly of ourselves, and we forget that we are mortal and accountable to Him who formed us from the dust of the earth. So easily and we think we are the ones in charge. We rob God of His Sovereignty.

Let's Pray: LORD God, we pray to You that help us in this endeavor and our lives. May we not become victims of those who have fallen into the trap of the enemy. Grace us with wisdom to know our insufficiency and cling solely to You. Help us so that we may not think as Saul thought and brought his kingdom to the ground. We bless you in Christ's name. Amen.

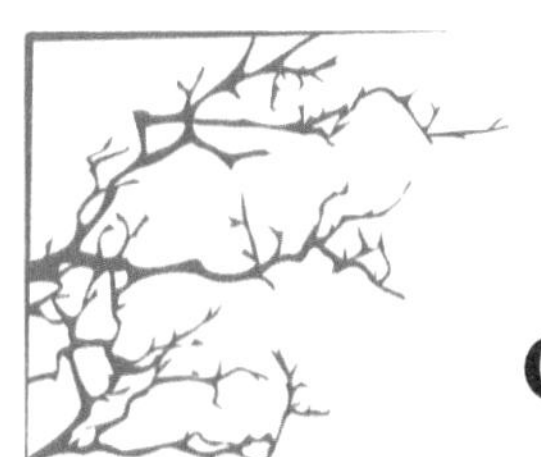

CHAPTER SIX

SIXTH CHARACTERS-—PHARISEES AND SADDUCEES
THE PHARISEES IN THEIR day were esteemed as holy men of God. They lived during a time when religion was the norm. They and the scribes together with the Sadducees were the great men of their time. They were the moral tutors for the people of Israel. The Pharisees taught the Bible and explained it to God's people every Sabbath. They were the teachers of the law. They were highly learned, people. Concerning the law, they knew it in depth.

The Pharisees thought they were far superior to others in this cause. They thought they were the ones who were special and were also closer to God because they ministered to God's people each day. The Pharisees undermined the common people and thought that they were holier than their countrymen. One of the Pharisees showed us what the Pharisees do in the week in these words: "I thank Thee that I am not like other people: swindlers, unjust, adulterers, or even like this tax-gatherer. 12 'I fast twice a week; I pay tithes of all that I get" (Luke 18:11-12NASB). The Pharisees fasted twice a week and paid tithes to the priests. They were the "spiritual" people of their time.

For this reason, they justified themselves before God. They dealt with their neighbors with contempt. They were not gracious to their brothers and fellow men. They were more concerned with the praise of men than the praise of God. They were more concerned with being spiritual than their neighbors. Their priority was not to know God better but rather to be better than their fellows. It is clear and evident that they were more concerned to justify themselves and condemn their brothers before God. After the Pharisee in the above text has justified himself, this happened to his fellow in the temple: "But the tax-gatherer, standing some distance away, was even unwilling to lift up his eyes to heaven, but was beating his breast, saying, 'God, be merciful to me, the sinner!'" (Luke 18:13 NASB).

Being holier than thou is never a good thing in the eyes of God. It is from the devil and the camp of the deceiver. The Pharisee, though he was the teacher of the law, was wrong about this. Though he thought that because of his act of piety, he was better than his brother, in the sight of God, pride is never better than anything and deserves condemnation. The Pharisee exalted himself and acted as though he deserved mercy. He thought he was holier than the commoner! As we have seen, the child of the spiritual than God is holier than thou; this continued in the life of the Pharisees.

The Pharisees laid a burden on people's necks, and yet they walk without having the same burden. They preached A and did B. They will preach mercy and act otherwise. This is their act of hypocrisy. Our Lord Jesus came to condemn them, and they were exasperated with Him. When the light of the gospel came, the law teachers couldn't lord over the people of God anymore. When Christ came, He posed a threat to their "holier than thou" mentality, and for this reason, they fought Him on every side. They did not want to see Him live. They wanted Him out of the way so that they could rule over people and continue their practice of "holier than thou" in their midst.

When the Pharisees wanted to lord over the people of God, the gospel came. The person of Christ Jesus is the embodiment of the gospel. He will not allow the Pharisees to continue down their road of hypocrisy. When the Pharisees were angry, they fought with Christ. Yes, it is their Christ for whom they fought. The Messiah was their Messiah. He was the one they had waited for so long. If the Pharisees had only stripped themselves of their pride and their act of holier than thou, they would not have proceeded to be more spiritual than God.

What did the early men of Israel hope for? Is it not the coming of the Messiah? Abraham, Isaac, Jacob, David, and the Prophets all believed, hoped, and even wrote about the coming Messiah! Yes, these people represent the law! This is what the Pharisees had been teaching their entire lives. They were law teachers, and because they were holier than thou, they overlooked Him so easily. The scripture says: Then a shoot will spring from the stem of Jesse, And a branch from his roots will bear fruit. **2** And the Spirit of the Lord will rest on Him, The spirit of wisdom and understanding, The spirit of counsel and strength, The spirit of knowledge and the fear of the Lord. **3** And He will delight in the fear of the Lord, And He will not judge by what His eyes see, Nor make a decision by what His ears hear; Isa 11:1-3NASB

Again it is said in another place: "You search the Scriptures, because you think that in them you have eternal life; and it is these that bear witness of Me; **40** and you are unwilling to come to Me, that you may have life" (John 5:39-40NASB). The branch in Isaiah 11 talks about Christ! It speaks of a man who will not judge by what he sees! It is He who delights in the fear of the Lord. He came and told the Pharisees that He was the Christ, but they did not listen because they were holier than thou. They wanted the glory of men, and they wanted to continue to receive their praise and high esteem.

For this reason, they rejected Christ. They persecuted Christ. Christ presented the gospel, and these Pharisees knew that their job was about to be taken away. They saw that their honor was about to be ripped off. The gospel cannot make any man glory in himself. The gospel only brings one to his knees, just as it brought the tax collector to acknowledge his utter insufficiency. Wasn't Apostle Paul a Pharisee? He said concerning his former days as a Pharisee: circumcised the eighth day, of the nation of Israel, of the tribe of Benjamin, a Hebrew of Hebrews; as to the Law, a Pharisee; **6** as to zeal, a persecutor of the church; as to the righteousness which is in the Law, found blameless. (Phil 3:5-6NASB). The one who said he was perfect in following the law and declared that he was righteous said later in his life after encountering the gospel: It is a trustworthy statement, deserving full acceptance, that Christ Jesus came into the world to save sinners, among whom I am foremost *of all*. (1 Tim 1:15NASB). You see, the one who was perfect as a Pharisee saw himself as the chief among sinners. If this is so, will the Pharisees in Jesus' time not reject Him? If the Pharisees of His time accepted Him, it meant only one thing—they would have also acknowledged their own insufficiency and the need for the cross.

This is what the Pharisees in Jesus' time couldn't afford. They were not ready to put their reputation aside. They wanted to continue to rule over people. How can they lord over people if they themselves are sinners and need the work of Christ to bring them into right standing with God? For this reason, they rejected Christ. When they rejected Christ, they said to the face of God that they were more spiritual than Him. What the Lord declared long ago about the coming Messiah, the Pharisees rejected! They threw the prophecy about the suffering Messiah in the bin and cherished the exalted Messiah! Yet in the knowledge of God, He saw fit to give mankind both the two works of the Messiah, one as the suffering servant and the other as the exalted king. This time, the Pharisees only accepted one and rejected the other. They thought they were more spiritual than God when they rejected the suffering Messiah. The Scripture talks about the Messiah, his coming, his work, and his exaltation, yet the Pharisees rejected Him because of their pride. They wanted the people to exalt them as though they were infallible, but they were fallible and also needed the grace of God.

When they rejected their Messiah, the Scripture recorded: "He came to His own, and those who were His own did not receive Him. **12** But as many as received Him, to them He gave the right to become children of God, *even* to those who believe in His name" (John 1:11-12NASB). His own people rejected Him! He brought light to illuminate the path of men, but they did not want the light. They were just okay with the darkness. The Pharisees rejected the Messiah and continued to justify themselves in the sight of God. Despite teaching and preaching the law, they did not see the one about whom the law was speaking. Paul was a former Pharisee; he wrote, "Therefore the Law has become our tutor *to lead us* to Christ, that we may be justified by faith" (Gal 3:24NASB). The law was given so that it would point men to Christ. How does it do that? It does that by showing man that he cannot please God in any way. The law silenced each man because all men fell short of what the law required.

For this reason, when all men failed to live up to the righteous standard of the law, men began to look forward to the deliverer. This is how the law pointed us to Christ. The law showed us our utter insufficiency! After our insufficiency is shown, we see that we need the Messiah! The Messiah came, and the Pharisees rejected and persecuted Him. It was not because the Pharisees were able to live up to the right standard of God's Law but rather on the contrary. They couldn't live up to the standard and yet wanted to behave as though they had been able to follow the law perfectly. When Christ came, they knew that their hypocrisy was going to be revealed by the light of Christ, and for this reason, they hated Him even more and crucified Him. In their case, being holier than thou led to being more spiritual than God. When the Pharisees rejected the Messiah, they said in their actions that they were more spiritual than God.

It was not only the Pharisees who behaved as though they were more spiritual than God but also, the Sadducees. The Sadducees were also leaders of the people of Israel. They were among the Sanhedrin! The chief priest was selected from the Sadducees. These people did not believe in the resurrection of the dead. They thought there was no resurrection after death and no hope after this life. As a result, they came to Jesus, attempting to push Him to falter. They asked Jesus this question, saying: "Teacher, Moses said, 'If a man dies, having no children, his brother as next of kin shall marry his wife, and raise up an offspring to his brother.' **25** "Now there were seven brothers with us; and the first married and died, and having no offspring left his wife to his brother; **26** so also the second, and the third, down to the seventh. **27** "And last of all, the woman died. **28** "In the resurrection therefore whose wife of the seven shall she be? For they all had her." **29** But Jesus answered and said to them, "You are mistaken, not understanding the Scriptures, or the power of God. **30** "For in the resurrection they neither marry, nor are given in marriage, but are like angels in heaven. **31** "But regarding the resurrection of the dead, have you not read that which was spoken to you by God, saying, **32** 'I am the God of Abraham, and the God of Isaac, and the God of Jacob'? He is not the God of the dead but of the living. Matt 22:24-32NASB. The answer that the Lord Jesus gave them silenced them once and for all concerning the resurrection of the dead. The God we worship is the God of the living, not the God of the dead. For this reason, those who have died are yet before Him. They are not asleep in spirit, as some even assume. They are asleep in the body but present before God.

Due to this, the Lord Jesus did not only confirm the resurrection of the dead but also silence his critics, who thought they knew better than God. They did that out of their ignorance of the word of God. They did not believe the Word of God because of their bias. It is the resurrection of the dead that separates the Pharisees from the Sadducees. The Pharisees believed in the resurrection of the dead, but the Sadducees did not. The Sadducees scorned the Pharisees because they believed that the dead would rise to life again. They laughed at them. They thought they were holier than them and knew better than them. This is what caused all the issues between the two leading groups in Israel.

Let's pray: Father, we thank You and praise Your glorious Name! We pray that You may help us so that our pride does not cloud our eyes from seeing You and giving ourselves wholeheartedly to You. Incline thy ears to hear our supplication and help us to not digress from the way of truth and liberty. Help us not to make the same mistakes as the Pharisees and Sadducees. May we not reject thy salvation, but rather assist us in cherishing thy Christ, whom You have given to us! We bless you in His name. Amen

CHAPTER SEVEN

SEVENTH CHARACTER-—JUDAS ISCARIOT

AS I SAID, AFTER THE fall of man, the posterity of man has always acted as though they were more spiritual than God. Judas, who was one of the twelve, is the next to be spoken about. Judas acted as though he were more spiritual than Christ, his master. The story narrates:

Mary therefore took a pound of very costly perfume of pure nard, and anointed the feet of Jesus, and wiped His feet with her hair; and the house was filled with the fragrance of the perfume. 4 But Judas Iscariot, one of His disciples, who was intending to betray Him, said, **5** "Why was this perfume not sold for three hundred denarii, and given to poor *people?*" **6** Now he said this, not because he was concerned about the poor, but because he was a thief, and as he had the money box, he used to pilfer what was put into it. John 12:3-6NASB

His act of piety is great if it wasn't a fabrication. He was thinking about charity, but what he was saying and what was in his heart was in opposition. He behaved as though he were the most spiritual apostle among the twelve, yet he was the worst. He was talking about charity, yet he was a thief. He was not thinking of anyone when he spoke of charity; he thought of himself and what he could have for himself. He did the math and saw that the perfume was worth a year's wages! He saw that the perfume was costly and could be a great gain if they only sold it and he kept the money. Judas, though he walked with Christ, did not convert from his foul ways, and in this act of behaving as though he were more spiritual than God, his identity was revealed. Each time this passage is read, the shame of Judas will be evident to all generations, unless this world passes away.

Maybe you are still waiting for me to reveal how Judas acted to demonstrate that he is more spiritual than God. I do wish to embark on that now! We should note that Christ Jesus, who is God Incarnate, never rejected it when the woman poured the perfume on Him. He welcomed it! It was only Judas who objected to that idea. Judas and Christ: who understands mercy, love, and compassion? This comparison should not even be made! In no way can Judas be compared to Christ. Christ is the compassionate God revealed in the flesh. And how dare Judas object if the God who has manifested Himself in the flesh has welcomed the use of perfume on Him?

In his act, Judas believed he was more spiritual than Christ. He thought he knew better and was holier than Christ. Selling to help the poor was Judas' idea. In this, he accuses Christ of accepting something that could have been used to show mercy and kindness to the poor. He accused the woman of not thinking about the poor and wasting her perfume on Jesus' feet! This was something Judas was not happy about. But the sad thing is that Judas was doing this in an act of hypocrisy. He had no poor in mind! He wanted the proceeds from the perfume.

Is this not a clear warning to us all? In our day, where many people take the things of God for granted and use godliness as a means of financial gain, is this not an alarm bell sounding in our ears? We are living in a day where many in their businesses are robbing their neighbors with higher margin profit percentages, which is unprecedented. We are in a season where the love of money has taken root among men. They speak as though they are spiritual, but deep within, they are robbing God. Some are robbing God in their giving!

They made vows and broke the vows and promises they had made to God. Judas spoke of something that made everyone assume he was spiritual, yet he was a robber. Are many not robbing their brothers and sisters? Are we not forsaking Christ and treasuring money? Instead of investing in the things of God, we do invest in the things that are frail and will pass away soon. Nonetheless, we speak as though we are spiritual men and women of God. Was the hypocrisy of Judas able to be hidden for long? Nay! His hypocrisy was manifest. We cannot assume to be more spiritual than God and yet live at liberty. Our vain spirituality and holier than thou always backfires.

We need to put a stop to hypocrisy and should not think that we know better than the King of kings and the Lord of lords. We should therefore be watchful that anything evil is not found in us. We should not be hasty to say all the good things with our lips if our heart is not with Christ. In this way, we can go about our lives while wearing hypocritical masks! This mask will be uncovered by the light of Christ. Was Judas able to hide behind that mask forever? Nay! The light of the Lord encased it! He was seen as he was.

It was because of the state of Judas' heart that Christ rebuked him for allowing the woman to use the perfume on Him. He who was able to read the intents of the heart, I believe, read the intents of Judas' heart and saw it as it was! What is the frame of our heart in God's eyes? Though we act as though we are pure, are we? Our acts of piety cannot stand up to the light of Christ if they are done in hypocrisy and folly. If we can say all the good things and live contrary to what our profession is, then we are living as though we are more spiritual than God. Did God ask us to profess and confess with our lips that we love Him? Isn't it true that God wants our hearts to do more of the talking by living holily and rightly? Does He not require us to love Him above all? This is where we mostly err!

In this day and age, profession has taken precedence over living a godly life. We do not see ourselves growing, living, and maturing in Christ, but we are growing in the profession, and our hearts continue to grow colder and colder. Judas, instead of loving God first above all things, tried to love man in the name of charity. Is this not what we are seeing in our day? Are they not robbing their customers? They do so in the name of helping God's work. They give a large sum of money to the advancement of God's work, but the source of their funds is evil.

Are some also not choosing their businesses over God? Are they not forsaking God in the name of chasing money? They are running after the wind and are chasing hard after what they will never have, namely, their shadows. If we continue on this path while also joining the multitudes in the house of God and acting spiritually, we should be aware that our hypocrisy will be exposed by the light of Christ soon to come unless we repent!

Let's Pray: Indeed, You are the sanctifier, Lord! We depend solely on You! Help us not to act as Judas did, who spoke in hypocrisy but not because he spoke from a good frame of mind and was moved by compassion towards the poor and the needy. Help us not to live the doppelgangers' lives; this we abhor! Help us that we may not wear masks, and help us that we may not forget ourselves because of the multitude we are in and think that we are Yours while we are far from You. So help us that we may not live our days walking and dining with You and Your people only in the flesh and yet walk and live far away from You and Your people in the heart. In Christ's name, we ask You for these things. Amen

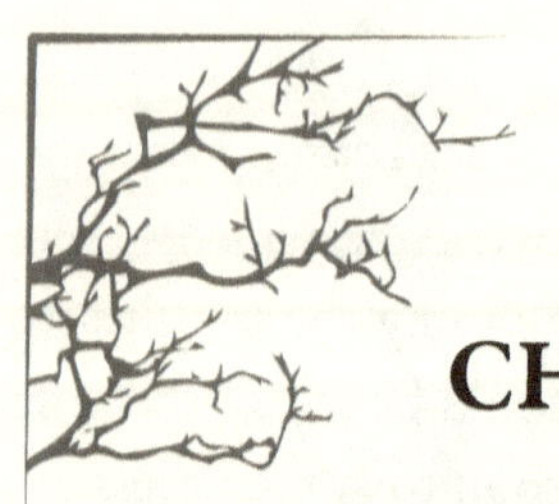

CHAPTER EIGHT

EIGHTH CHARACTER-—SIMON PETER

And on the next day, as they were on their way, and approaching the
city, Peter went up on the housetop about the sixth hour to pray. **10**
And he became hungry, and was desiring to eat; but while they were
making preparations, he fell into a trance; **11** and he beheld the sky
opened up, and a certain object like a great sheet coming down, lowered
by four corners to the ground, **12** and there were in it all *kinds of*
four-footed animals and crawling creatures of the earth and birds of the
air. **13** And a voice came to him, "Arise, Peter, kill and eat!" **14** But Peter
said, "By no means, Lord, for I have never eaten anything unholy and
unclean." **15** And again a voice *came* to him a second time, "What God
has cleansed, no *longer* consider unholy." **16** And this happened three
times; and immediately the object was taken up into the sky. **17** Now
while Peter was greatly perplexed in mind Acts 10:9-17NASB

GOD WAS DOING SOMETHING new in the history of mankind!
After the fall of man, God purported to deal with only a chosen remnant.
These people were called the Israelites. The Israelites descended from
Noah through Shem, Abraham, Isaac, and Jacob. God chose this line
and dealt specifically with them. When God chose the Israelites, He
told them what types of animals they should eat and what they should
not. When our Lord Jesus came, something new was about to happen.
God was not going to deal with only the Israelites but rather the entire
human race, language, and color. Eating food or meat no longer mattered
in this context. The eating of some specific foods was to distinguish
the Israelites from the rest of the world, but since the time of the New
Covenant, God was going to deal with the whole posterity of Adam.

Whether the person is African, Asian, European, or American, God is about to do something with his life.

This is where Peter tried to be more spiritual than God. When the meal descended from above, Peter knew that it was from God, yet he chose not to eat. Was Peter thinking that God was asking him to eat something that He had forbidden them to eat? Wasn't it God who said they couldn't eat? If the same Lord provides it to Peter, does he object and reject what God has sanctified? This is the error that we make! We easily box God into our theological positions because of His previous acts! We try to keep Him in our cage, and when He gets out, we become frustrated. Easily, we forget Him who is the immutable and omnipotent God.

Peter, when he refused to eat the food, was holding on to the old way that God dealt with the posterity of Adam. The New Covenant was bringing Adam's descendants, who have wallowed in sin and confusion, into God's family. They were being welcomed into the family of Christ. This is what Peter misinterpreted, and it is why he acted as if he were more spiritual than God. Not only was Peter refusing to eat, but he was also missing God's shift in how He deals with man. This was what Peter failed to grasp!

God has written a new chapter in the history of mankind. The lost sheep has now been found. God is not dealing with only part of the world now! He is now dealing with the entire world. He is not a respecter of persons; if you repent and trust Him, He will not cast you out! The lost wanderer has now returned. What did Jesus say to the Canaanite woman when the woman said: "Have mercy on me, O Lord, Son of David; my daughter is cruelly demon-possessed." **23** But He did not answer her a word. And His disciples came to *Him* and kept asking Him, saying, "Send her away, for she is shouting out after us." **24** But He answered and said, "I was sent only to the lost sheep of the house of Israel." **25** But she came and *began* to bow down before Him, saying, "Lord, help me!" **26** And He answered and said, "It is not good to take the children's bread and throw it to the dogs." **27** But she said, "Yes, Lord; but even the dogs feed on the crumbs which fall from their masters' table" (Matt 15:22-27 NASB). The woman was likened to a dog! The gentile nations were also likened to the pigs that the Israelites were prohibited from eating. God has now united the gentile nations! The Lord does not only meet His people in Jerusalem but everywhere! Those who worship God in truth are the true people of God. It is not the sons of Jacob alone that are the people of God, but rather all flesh. The door is open. The veil has been torn asunder. Salvation is available to anyone who believes. This is what God was doing when He showed Peter the food that he rejected!

Let's Pray: Father, to You, do we ascribe all praise and honor!" We beseech You, Lord, to give us understanding and to illumine our minds so that we can comprehend Your truth in simplicity. So that we do not fight thy will for mankind and can do what thou hast predestined for us to do. We bless You in Christ. Amen

CHAPTER NINE

NINTH CHARACTER-—UNREGENERATE MAN

WHEN THE PEOPLE OF Israel rejected Christ, His name was sent to the gentile nations! When it got there, the posterity of Adam continued to harden their hearts. The way of salvation is being made known, and the door thereof has been opened wide, but the stiff-necked will not come to Christ. In this regard, many who are in the world rejected Christ on the basis of impossibility. What I mean is that, when Christ was revealed to them, many said in their hearts that it was a fabrication. Many people believed that the resurrection of Christ was a story and a fantasy made up by some people.

In this, man professed to be more spiritual than God. This is because man decided not to follow God's only way to salvation. Rather than following God's way, man is scheming his own way to redeem himself from the power of sin. The fallen man has rejected the rest and peace of Christ. The fallen man has been blinded into thinking that he is pleasing God. The devil is still working, and he has trapped many a soul with his delusion.

Why are so many rejecting the Christian faith? Is it not because the enemy, called Satan, is still blinding them from seeing the truth? Simple logic and critical analysis should have sent many to the Bible! Is it not surprising that the Bible has stood the test of time and passed? The Bible was written by more than forty authors, many of whom did not know each other. Writing took a thousand and five hundred years! It was written on three different continents, namely, Asia, Africa, and Europe.

It was not just one individual who sat at some place to record his private revelations, but rather more than forty men wrote the Bible, yet the Bible is cohesive and true, and the archaeological dates in the Bible have been proven to be true over and over again. The New Testament was written by men in the first century who were witnesses or companions of the witnesses to the life and ministry of Christ. They saw it all and recorded it as it is!

Many assume that the Christian faith is a fabrication of lies and tales, of which Constantine is the father. Those who say such a thing are, in fact, ignorant of history. They are also ignorant of facts. This is, the Christian faith is not something that man can even fabricate. Constantine won his war and became emperor of Rome in 313 A.D. Before Constantine came, the church had been suffering from persecution for three centuries already. Many of the church fathers have already been martyred! The apostles have all died! The Bible has already been written. Sixty-six books have already been designated as the Christian Bible.

It was not the church fathers who wrote the Bible. It was the Apostles and their close companions. When Constantine came, the Christian Bible was already there! The sixty-six books were already in use. It was not only in use; it had also spread to the entire Roman Empire and other vicinities! Ignatius, Polycarp, Irenaeus, Clement of Rome, Clement of Alexandria, and more of the church fathers who lived in different places already had the Bible. They not only had the Bible but also quoted it many times in their writings. Justin Martyr has already written his apologetics!

You see, before Constantine came, this is what happened. To say that Constantine altered the Word of God is to speak of your own ignorance. If he altered the Word that was in their possession in the Roman capital, he could not have done so to that which was in the possession of the Alexandrian church in Egypt. Neither could they have altered the Asian Bible. Many in their day have already been exposed to the truth of the Bible, and they have been talking about it for more than three hundred years. The Bible has also been translated from Greek and Hebrew. Constantine would have to go for all those translations and retranslate them!

And again, Constantine would have to go for all the writings of the church fathers and retranslate all the Bible quotes in their writings. This is what many are saying! They are saying this is what Constantine did! Do you now understand why I say that they are ignorant of history and facts if they say that the Christian Bible has been corrupted by Constantine? Enough of this; let me continue my discussion!

If the Bible is correct, and it is! So, why don't men believe what the Bible says about the Savior? Why do men still follow their own ways? If the Bible says that Jesus is the only way, then why do men not believe? Why do men put their trust in the private revelation of someone whose end is unknown? Are men not telling God that they are more spiritual than him? If men were not telling God that they were more spiritual than Him, they would have turned to the cross of Christ for salvation. Why are many not embracing the Christian religion? In the face of all these facts that Christ has come, died, and risen, why are men rejecting him? Men are not running to Christ! If Jesus is the only Savior, and He is, why then do men not run to Him? Are men not saying with their lives that they are more spiritual than God for bringing Christ into the world and making Him the only way to eternal rest?

What does the Scripture say? "And there is salvation in no one else; for there is no other name under heaven that has been given among men, by which we must be saved." (Acts 4:12NASB). There are no alternatives; there is only one! You must either enter the narrow path or die! It is clear that all those who reject Him will suffer harm, yet men are not running to Christ! Men are going back and forth, hoping to be saved at the end! Is this not more spiritual than God? The God whom many believe they are worshiping has revealed his plan to man, yet he is rejecting it! The Lord has revealed His plan in Christ Jesus as the only way to salvation, yet many are not turning to faith in Him and yet expect to be saved at last!

Now, even now, this pandemic is with us. Christ is far from the lives of many, and they think they will make it to heaven at last. Who gave them that assurance? Are they not giving false assurances? Are they not saying that they are more spiritual than God? Did God not see many ways and yet declare that it is only in Christ that salvation is guaranteed? If this is so, why then are men saying that all roads lead to Rome? Why are they claiming that God will accept them if they reject Christ as the world's savior? They are behaving as though they know better than God and yet expect to obey Him. They have created their religions and their dos and don'ts, and yet they think that they will be accepted by God at last! The scripture expressly says:

"For God so loved the world, that He gave His only begotten Son, that whoever believes in Him should not perish, but have eternal life. **17** "For God did not send the Son into the world to judge the world, but that the world should be saved through Him. **18** "He who believes in Him is not judged; he who does not believe has been judged already, because he has not believed in the name of the only begotten Son of God. **19** "And this is the judgment, that the light is come into the world, and men loved the darkness rather than the light; for their deeds were evil. **20** "For everyone who does evil hates the light, and does not come to the light, lest his deeds should be exposed. **21** "But he who practices the truth comes to the light, that his deeds may be manifested as having been wrought in God." John 3:16-21NASB

Those who have rejected the light are those who say that they are more spiritual than God. They are saying that they do not need the light of God before they will see! They are saying that without Christ they can live and manage to enter God's rest, for all roads lead to Rome. Is this not saying that you are more spiritual than God? Did God not see you in the darkness and send you His light? If you were already in the light, would God have sent you the eternal light? In this light is life! In this light, there is liberty! To reject this light is to reject salvation. Why then does the fallen man continue to reject the only light and yet manage to accuse God of unfaithfulness? Are they not saying that they are more spiritual than God? Are they not justifying themselves? For this reason, the scripture says: "For the wrath of God is revealed from heaven against all ungodliness and unrighteousness of men, who suppress the truth in unrighteousness" (Rom 1:18NASB).

The wrath of God is coming upon them, and it will not tarry. God will send them a great delusion since they have assumed that they are more spiritual than He is. In their act of ignorance, they have rejected Christ. In God's anger, He will send them a great delusion to believe what is false. They will fight for what is false. Will you not take the road of deception and fight against the path of folly if you believe you are more spiritual than God? Is Satan still not fighting God despite all the doom that awaits him?

This is how God's delusion is likened to the one He sends on those who harden their hearts. This is how these people, who have rejected Christ and created many roads for themselves, are compared! They are treading on a road that does not end. There is no guarantee of rest for their souls. They are going farther and farther from Christ. If the unregenerate do not turn to Christ, alas, doom will clothe him all the days that he will live on earth. He will not only suffer harm in this land but also in the next.

They should know that they cannot be more spiritual than the Omnipotent God. They should know that there is only one way to salvation. There is no hope of salvation apart from Christ. This is what an unregenerate man should know. Why is the unregenerate scorning the only option? Why do the unregenerate scorn and mock the Christian faith, which is the only religion ordained by God? Because of the reliability of both the Old and New Testaments, the Christian faith is the only remedy. The Bible has been proven to be God's word.

Those who claim that they hold the original word of God cannot help themselves, except they consult the Bible, which contains sixty-six books! Is this not surprising? How can some men claim to hold the true word of God and yet consult the Bible if they believe it has been adulterated? Is this not a contradiction? Believers in the body of Christ only need the Bible alone. We need no supplements, which are also infallible. There is only one infallible book that God has given to us, and it is the Bible. Those who accuse are the ones who use it the most.

They quote the Scriptures daily to preach to their people and yet claim that the Bible has been corrupted. If they accept that the Bible is not corrupted, they would have to agree that it is only Jesus Christ who is the only way to the Father, which they cannot accept, and for that reason, they have to say the Bible is corrupted. Yet, they have failed to neglect the Bible outright. They cannot live and feed on their holy book, except to consult the Bible. This demonstrates how powerful God's book has been and continues to be.

The Bible has stated time and again that Christ Jesus is the only way to heaven. To believe that all religion leads to heaven is to be a stranger to God's infallible Word. There is no obscurity in this. If something is obscure in the Bible, it is not the doctrine of soteriology. That is, Jesus is clearly and emphatically the only way, as Peter stated in Acts 4, verse 12. To say otherwise is to think that you are more spiritual than God! If you claim to be spiritual, God will allow you to fight for the wrong cause due to the delusion He will send your way. This is why I do wish to call my brothers who are fighting a religious battle and defending something contrary to the Bible, that they should come to the Bible in humility and examine the facts presented by the Scripture for their own sake.

I plead with the conscience of my reader that he should resolve at once to renounce anything contrary to the Bible and cling to the Christian faith. We should run from folly to Christ, who is the wisdom and power of God. My faithful reader should examine the facts I have laid out in this chapter about the Bible and see whether they are true. Why don't you believe the Bible if all of this is true? Why do you make God a liar and make man true? So, why do you place more faith in religion than in God? I leave this for your own answer! Do not injure your immortal soul with your religion, which cares more about what religious leaders have to say than what God has to say. Come at once to the cross and repent in ashes. Embrace the cross of Christ for your own soul's sake!

Let's Pray: Lord, not to us, not to us, but to thy name we give all glory. We pray that help us and deliver us from folly. Father, remove the specks and scales from our eyes so that we may see and know you. Anoint our eyes to see and appreciate your splendor. Help us to trust only in the cross of Christ and the work that He has wrought on our behalf. We bless you in His Name. Amen

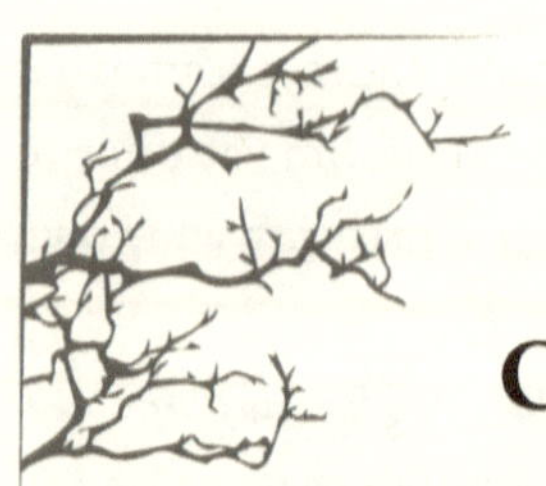

CHAPTER TEN

FINAL CHARACTER-—SOME MINISTERS

I ALWAYS SAY THAT FAITHFUL ministers are one of the best gifts God has given mankind throughout history. From the Old to the New Testaments, there is one thing that God continues to do. It is faithful ministers that He sends to His people. It is such a blessing to hear God's word preached to you with such simplicity. Hearing words from the pulpit exalting Christ and rebuking sin, the flesh, and fleshly deeds is a great privilege for us if our souls are to be saved.

In this gospel age, we have seen many faithful ministers of the gospel who have done God's work faithfully and are even doing so in our day. Many have renounced the deeds of the flesh as a result of faithful preachers; many have fallen in love with Christ; and many are now in a relationship with the true God, who revealed Himself to this world in the Person of Christ Jesus. God has drawn men to Himself because of faithful ministers. That is God's way of drawing men to Himself.

Our Lord Jesus in the New Testament was such a great preacher who preached from His heart and the love He has for souls. It was our Lord Jesus who preached, and we saw the importance of a single soul. Our Lord made us know that a single soul saved is worth the whole earth. Through his preaching, God turned the hearts of men toward himself. When He was ascending to heaven, He gave his power to His apostles for the furtherance of the work of salvation. Peter rose and preached on the day of Pentecost, and on that day, three thousand souls were turned to Christ.

Faithful ministers have done much more good to the kingdom of God than we think. They have been a great blessing to God's kingdom.

They have brought many a wandering soul home into a relationship with God. God always uses them to bring men to Himself. This is why we cannot take it for granted if God gives us a faithful minister who exposes God's word and His truth to our hearing. It is the Word that is able to save our souls and bring us back from the road of many sorrows.

After all that I have said above, there is something we are taking for granted in our generation. Looking at where sermons are going in our day and age is heartbreaking and pathetic. The faithful ministers are declining each day. The number of those who still hold to the simplicity of the gospel is small! The seriousness with which we should approach this issue should not be questioned.

We have arrived at an era where many preachers think that they are more spiritual than Christ. When our Lord came, He preached about hell more than anyone in the history of man during His day. Now we have many who are saying that preaching hell and sin is not necessary. They do profess that if we preach the love of God, it will draw more men to Christ than hell and sin. For this reason, we have many people filling our churches, yet they live godlessly and immorally.

Consecration is departing from our churches daily. The name of our Lord is being blasphemed among those who do not believe. The gospel is being scorned by them. They think the power of God to save has lost its energy and efficacy. They heard that the gospel saves, but they see from the lives of many professing Christians that they are living as strangers to the cross. They witness their lives, and from this, they have concluded that the Christian message about the cross of Christ is not efficacious. Isn't this heartbreaking, Sirs? If this is not the case, then what is? Do we give men an opportunity to doubt the gospel? Do we go around giving false assurance to people that they are saved while their lives are contrary to their profession? To guarantee the salvation of someone who lives in habitual sin is to profess that you are more spiritual than God.

Motivational speaking does not draw men to Christ but rather draws them to the podium, not the cross. It allows those who have not repented to think they are saved when they are not. What type of love do we preach to people if God's judgment against sin is not preached? What type of assurance do we give to people who think that God is not just? If God is only love, then He cannot be just to these people. Will they not continue in their foul ways and yet claim that they can walk in uncleanliness and filthiness and yet be saved? Sirs, I do wish to ask you these questions.

Does the Bible not say that: "But God demonstrates His own love toward us, in that while we were yet sinners, Christ died for us" (Rom 5:8-9NASB)? Is not the love of God seen in His justice? Because of the justice of God, Christ died. If the Son of God died because of sin, do we, therefore, assume that sin is a small enemy? Is it not sin that made the Son of God cry, "My God, My God, why have you forsaken me?" Is it not sin that made Him shout, "I thirst?" Is it not sin that put nails in His hands and feet? Is it not sin that thrust and pierce His side with a dagger? Do we assume that sin should not be preached and revealed as it is? To say this is to think you are more spiritual than God.

Didn't the Apostle preach Christ and His crucifixion? If we do not preach the penalty that Christ paid on the cross, can we estimate His love for us? If we do not preach hell and the fury of God's anger against all those who live and enjoy sin, how can they measure the love of God for them? This is not the time for some ministers to boast and give ideas as though they are more spiritual than God. We have seen many who have gone down the path of being more spiritual than God, and we have seen their tragic ends. We need no more! With urgency, we need to address this error. Many a soul is at risk. God draws men to Himself through faithful preaching, but if preaching is corrupted, many a soul will be damned. If those who profess to be saved live and walk in habitual sin, should we not see that our ideologies are wrong?

For this reason, I call to the attention of all faithful preachers of the gospel that they need to stand for God even more in this adulterous generation. Apostle Paul said: "For I am not ashamed of the gospel, for it is the power of God for salvation to everyone who believes" (Rom 1:16NASB). It is the gospel alone, preached in its simplicity, that is the power of God to bring salvation. The truth of God should be spoken, sirs. The cross must be preached once again. As in the days of old, sin must be spoken against. If men will be damned, we should not help them. If men will perish and go to hell, we should not give them a reason to continue on their path. If men will die in their sins, we should not help them with fables and cunning. Let's preach the truth in simplicity, for it is in it that souls are saved!

If we do not preach the justice of God, then we are preaching an unbalanced message; it does not matter the good frame of our hearts. Yes, the love of God must be preached, but we should know that the love of God is revealed to mankind more clearly in His justice and judgment against sin. Christ did not die because He was pleased with death. He was sorrowful and in great anguish in Gethsemane; do we assume it was funny for Him? He cried out that He would avoid the hostility and humiliation that were coming His way. He still died for our sins because of His love. He knew that if we lived in habitual sins, we would die. And He knew that if He did not intervene, we would have no option other than to perish in our sins. This is the reason He went to the cross—that we might not continue in sin. He went to the cross to take away the power of sin. The power of sin was nullified by the blood of Christ. It is now possible to live in holiness. It was not so in the beginning.

Do we, therefore, play with the souls of many people because we want to be more spiritual than God? May it not be so. This is high time that faithful ministers should arise and oppose the consumer sermons that men are preaching to us in our day. May we not fall for the fanciful stories of those who say preaching about hell and sin is not loving. Are we to love God or not? Are we not to love our neighbors after our love has been demonstrated toward God? If we love men, do we, therefore, hide the truth from them? If we love God, do we preach His truth with prejudice and unfairness? I'll leave it to your conscience to decide!

May we not be more spiritual than our Lord, who preached about sin and hell. May we not try to be holier than the apostles who preached and wrote about sin and hell. Do we now preach earthly prosperity to people and neglect heavenly prosperity? Oh, how sad and pathetic our generation is! Will the apostles not weep and cry because of how we have fallen to earth? When Paul laid all that he had down for the necessity of knowing Christ, now we preach to people to go for what Paul has laid down. You see, Paul laid down his certificate as a Pharisee; now we cherish it more than Christ. Paul laid down what in our day will be called a "green card" as a citizen of Rome for the necessity of knowing Christ. What do we see in our days? Many preachers preach that people will go abroad and enjoy life, and for this reason, Christ is not treasured. Lies are what have encompassed our embassies! They lie about their age, identity, and marriage in the name of traveling abroad. Paul laid down his treasures upon the face of the earth; for the necessity of having more treasures in the New City, what about us? We treasure money, fame, and buildings more than we treasure Christ.

How did this all begin? Did it not begin when prosperity preachers came to the scene? O, sirs, should we not weep on the harm we have caused this generation with our silence? Should we not stand up now and preach like never before because of these souls we have kept quiet for them to perish? Are we now becoming wicked shepherds who do not care about the flocks of Christ that are falling prey to these wolves? Should we not be as David when he said: "When a lion or a bear came and took a lamb from the flock, **35** I went out after him and attacked him, and rescued *it* from his mouth; and when he rose up against me, I seized *him* by his beard and struck him and killed him. **36** Your servant has killed both the lion and the bear; and this uncircumcised Philistine will be like one of them, since he has taunted the armies of the living God." (1 Sam 17:34-36NASB). Should we not be as he was and take God's flocks from the mouths of the wolves in our generation who are damning many a soul to hell with their tales, fanciful stories, and dreams? Should we not fight Goliath if we want God's people to be at liberty?

O, faithful preachers, arise on your feet once again! The banner with the inscription "the gospel of Christ" should be preached once again. Let us fight wolves if we want to keep the sheep safe. Those who are more spiritual than God will definitely fight our message, but it is what our Lord preached and His apostles too. As a result, we should follow in their footsteps. When you do that, you will be in good company. We should fight the battle they themselves fought with all our strength. The coming of our Christ is imminent, and jokes, tales, and storytelling in the house of God are enough. Let's return to the basics in Christ if we want our souls and the souls of our hearers saved.

Let's pray: Gracious Father, give us confidence and boldness to stand for Your truth. Christ and His apostles preached for man's salvation. Help us so that we will not preach to tickle the ears of our hearers. Help us not to become entertainers and neglect our duty as watchmen who are accountable for souls. Thank you for hearing us. Amen.

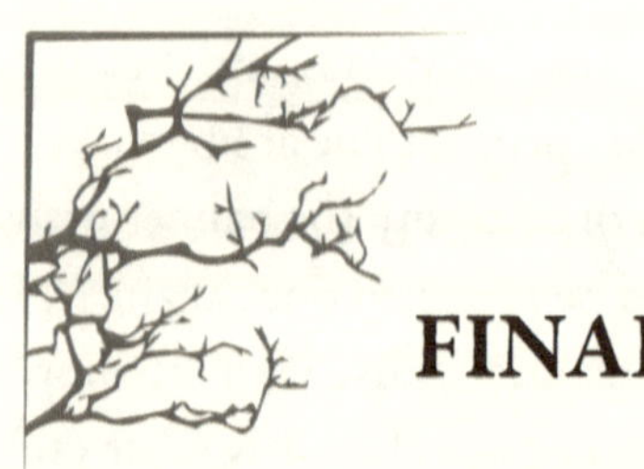

FINAL SUMMARY

THE BOOK AND YOU

WE HAVE ENDED OUR JOURNEY, and I believe you have not wasted your precious time going through this short discourse. We thank God for that.

After a successful journey, we have seen how spiritual than God started when Lucifer coveted the place of God and ruined his own self. The first parents of mankind also behaved as though they were more spiritual than their Creator by going after what they have not been given, and they injured their souls. Henceforth, holier than thou was born when our first parents tried to play the blame game. These two characters have haunted the posterity of man to our day. Each day, we are faced with many decisions, and it boils down to whether we are more spiritual than God and are holier than our brothers or not! Each decision we make shows whether we are God's people or we live for ourselves. If we do not belong to God, it means that we want to be like God as Satan did.

This book was written so that many will be conscious of the battle we are fighting and will be wise in this battle. We need to examine and reexamine our lives to see if any foul ways are in our hearts and lives! Easily, and the heart of man puffs up. For this cause, we need to check daily to see that we are God's people.

Specifically speaking, I do want all brothers and sisters in the body of Christ who are preachers to know what they are up against. They should not back down now, and as they have done previously with the grace of God on their lives, they should do more even now. What they are doing for the Lord is never in vain. They should go on working with the strength that God has provided for them. They should not linger nor hesitate but rather be resolved at once to give their best to Christ in this fight. Sirs, we are going home very soon, and this is the most needful time in the history of man that the battle has been more intense, and this is when Christ needs His army to fight. Let us therefore put on the armor, whether it be the armor of a godly man or the armor of a Christian soldier. God bless you and increase you greatly. Amen.

Works Cited

Nelson, T. (2002). *NKJV, New Spirit-Filled Life Bible, eBook: Kingdom Equipping Through the Power of the Word*. Thomas Nelson.

Don't miss out!

Visit the website below and you can sign up to receive emails whenever Michael Yaw Tano publishes a new book. There's no charge and no obligation.

https://books2read.com/r/B-A-ESQH-KIBGC

BOOKS 2 READ

Connecting independent readers to independent writers.

About the Author

Michael Yaw Tano is a young man who loves the Lord. He is an Assemblies of God minister. Currently, he serves as the Associate Pastor at Calvary Hill Chapel, Asokore Mampong. He also loves to read the Puritans and the reformers. Michael has a passion for writing. He loves to talk about his risen Christ and to learn of Him each day. Since he met the Lord Jesus, his life has changed completely and his affections and desires are to do the work of God and to give his very best to Christ who so went to the cross for him. This is his motivation in life, that is, to live each day serving the Lord with all his might. He holds a Diploma of Divinity and Associates of Divinity degree from Christian Leaders College (USA) and Bachelor of Religious Studies together with Graduate Certificate in Biblical Studies from Nations University (USA). He is pursuing a Master of Theological Studies at Nations University.

You can contact him on:
Email: tanomichael65@gmail.com
Phone: +233542443585

Read more at https://www.miketano.wordpress.com.